BLESS
PRAYER BOOK

Edited by Bart Tesoriero

Illustrations by Michael Adams

Nihil Obstat: Right Reverend Archimandrite Francis Vivona, S.T.M., J.C.L.

Imprimatur: Most Reverend Joseph A. Pepe, D.D., J.C.D.

Date: November 18, 2008
        Dedication of the Basilicas of Saints Peter and Paul

Library of Congress Control Number: 2011910838
ISBN 1-936020-40-9
© 2008 by Aquinas Press
Eleventh Printing, January, 2017

TABLE OF CONTENTS

INTRODUCTION

"Come to me, all you who labor and are burdened,
and I will give you rest."
—Matthew 11:28

God loves you! He created you, and each of us, with a God-sized hole in our hearts, so that we would always long for someone to truly love us, fill us, and in whom we could finally find rest. When our first parents lost their original communion with God in Paradise, He did not abandon them. Rather, in an excess of passion and devotion, through the sacrifice of His own Son, God restored our fellowship and brought us into an even more intimate communion with Himself, a communion that is destined to end in our being made totally one with Him eternally in heaven. That's *Amazing Grace!*

We have written this book to help you come to Jesus, who is present most excellently in the Blessed Sacrament, that you might love Him, adore Him, and comfort Him for all the suffering He endured to save you. It is our hope that these prayers, devotions, and meditations might also help you receive the grace of His life in return — eternal, satisfying, rejuvenating, healing, cleansing, strengthening, and power-imparting life!

This book includes prayers before and after Communion; prayers and meditations for Eucharistic devotions such as Benediction, Holy Hours, and Visits to the Blessed Sacrament; Scripture readings, litanies, and more.

In his first encyclical, *Deus Caritas Est*, Pope Benedict XVI teaches that true communion with Jesus always "spills out into acts of love for others." He asserts that our mission as Christians ought never be separated from our holiness, because our gift to the world is God Himself. In order to allow God the opportunity to fill us, transform us, and "divinize" us, we need to spend time apart with Him, to receive what Archbishop Fulton J. Sheen called "divine radiation."

May God grant you holiness, grace, peace, and serenity in the quiet hours you spend "alone with the Alone" in the liturgy, in Eucharistic devotions, and in adoration of Jesus. As Pope Saint John Paul II exhorted us, "May our adoration never cease."

MORNING PRAYER

The Sign of the Cross

In the name of the Father, ✠ and of the Son, and of the Holy
Spirit. Amen.

Our Father

Our Father, Who art in heaven, hallowed be Thy name.
Thy kingdom come, Thy will be done,
on earth as it is in heaven.
Give us this day our daily bread;
and forgive us our trespasses,
as we forgive those who trespass against us;
and lead us not into temptation,
but deliver us from evil. Amen.

Hail Mary

Hail Mary, full of grace, the Lord is with thee.
Blessed art thou among women,
and blessed is the fruit of thy womb, Jesus.
Holy Mary, Mother of God, pray for us sinners,
now and at the hour of our death. Amen.

Glory be to the Father

Glory be to the Father, and to the Son, and to the Holy Spirit;
as it was in the beginning, is now, and ever shall be, world
without end. Amen.

Morning Offering to the Sacred Heart

O Jesus, through the Immaculate Heart of Mary,
I offer You my prayers, works, joys, and sufferings of this day,
in union with the Holy Sacrifice of the Mass offered
throughout the world, in reparation for all my sins,
for all the intentions of Your Sacred Heart, and in particular for
the intentions of our Holy Father. Amen.

Daily Consecration to Mary

O Mary, my Queen and my Mother,
I give myself entirely to you.
And as proof of my filial devotion,
I consecrate to you this day
my eyes, my ears, my mouth, my heart,
my whole being without reserve.
Wherefore, good Mother,
As I am your own,
Keep me and guard me
As your property and possession. Amen.

Guardian Angel Prayer

O Angel of God, my Guardian dear,
To whom God's love, commits me here;
Ever this day, be at my side,
To light and guard, to rule and guide. Amen.

EVENING PRAYER

Come, Holy Spirit, fill the hearts of Your faithful,
and enkindle in us the fire of Your divine Love.
Send forth Your Spirit and we shall be created,
and You shall renew the face of the earth.

Let us pray: O God, who by the light of Your Holy Spirit, has
instructed the hearts of Your faithful, grant us by the same
Spirit to be truly wise and ever to rejoice in His consolation,
through the same Christ our Lord. Amen.

*Take a moment to review your day. Thank God for the good things that
have happened, and ask His forgiveness for any times you have failed to
love Him or others.*

Dear God, thank You for keeping me safe today and for giving
me so many blessings and graces. Please forgive all my sins and
fill me with Your love. Give me and those I love a restful sleep.
Through the intercession of our Blessed Mother Mary, good
Saint Joseph, and all the angels and saints, have mercy on us,
that we may arise with renewed faith, hope, and love. Amen.

Visit this house, we pray you, O Lord.
Drive far away from us all the snares of the enemy.
May Your holy angels stay here and guard us in peace,
and let Your blessing be always upon us.
Through Christ our Lord. Amen.

Nunc Dimittis
The Song of Simeon

Antiphon: Save us, Lord, while we are awake; and protect us while we sleep; that we may keep watch with Christ and rest with Him in peace.

"Now, Master, you may let your servant go
   in peace, according to your word,
for my eyes have seen your salvation,
   which you prepared in sight of all the peoples,
a light for revelation to the Gentiles,
   and glory for your people Israel." —LUKE 2:29-32

Glory be to the Father, and to the Son, and to the Holy Spirit;
as it was in the beginning, is now, and ever shall be,
world without end. Amen.

Watch, O Lord, with those who wake,
or watch, or weep tonight,
and give Your Angels and Saints charge over those who sleep.
Tend Your sick ones, O Lord Christ.
Rest Your weary ones,
Bless Your dying ones,
Soothe Your suffering ones,
Pity Your afflicted ones,
Shield Your joyous ones,
And all for Your love's sake. Amen. —SAINT AUGUSTINE

May the Lord grant us a peaceful night and a perfect end.
Amen.

PREPARATION FOR HOLY COMMUNION

Psalm 84

How lovely your dwelling,
O LORD of hosts!
My soul yearns and pines
for the courts of the LORD.
My heart and flesh cry out
for the living God.

As the sparrow finds a home
and the swallow a nest to settle her young,
My home is by your altars,
LORD of hosts, my king and my God!
Happy are those who dwell in your house!
They never cease to praise you.
Happy are those who find refuge in you,
whose hearts are set on pilgrim roads.
As they pass through the Baca valley,
they find spring water to drink.
Also from pools the Lord provides water
for those who lose their way.
They pass through outer and inner wall
and see the God of gods on Zion.
LORD of hosts, hear my prayer;
listen, God of Jacob.
O God, look kindly on our shield;
look upon the face of your anointed.
Better one day in your courts
than a thousand elsewhere.
Better the threshold of the house of my God
than a home in the tents of the wicked.
For a sun and shield is the LORD God,
bestowing all grace and glory.
The LORD withholds no good thing
from those who walk without reproach.
O LORD of hosts,
happy are those who trust in you!

Psalm 116

I love the LORD, who listened
to my voice in supplication,
Who turned an ear to me
on the day I called.
I was caught by the cords of death;
the snares of Sheol had seized me;
I felt agony and dread.
Then I called on the name of the LORD,
"O LORD, save my life!"
Gracious is the LORD and just;
yes, our God is merciful.
The LORD protects the simple;
I was helpless, but God saved me.
Return, my soul, to your rest;
the LORD has been good to you.
For my soul has been freed from death,
my eyes from tears, my feet from stumbling.
I shall walk before the LORD
in the land of the living.
I kept faith, even when I said,
"I am greatly afflicted!"
I said in my alarm,
"No one can be trusted!"
How can I repay the LORD
for all the good done for me?
I will raise the cup of salvation
and call on the name of the LORD.

I will pay my vows to the LORD
in the presence of all his people.
Too costly in the eyes of the LORD
is the death of his faithful.
LORD, I am your servant,
your servant, the child of your maidservant;
you have loosed my bonds.
I will offer a sacrifice of thanksgiving
and call on the name of the LORD.
I will pay my vows to the LORD
in the presence of all his people,
In the courts of the house of the LORD,
in your midst, O Jerusalem.
Hallelujah!

A Song of Thanksgiving

Give thanks to the LORD, who is good,
whose love endures forever.
Let the house of Israel say:
God's love endures forever.
Let the house of Aaron say,
God's love endures forever.
Let those who fear the LORD say,
God's love endures forever.
You are my God, I give you thanks;
my God, I offer you praise.
—PSALM 118:1-4; 28

JESUS COMES IN THE MORNING

Cardinal Henry Edward Manning

*Early in the morning,
Jesus stood on the shore.*
—JOHN 21:4 (NIV)

Each day begins with the presence of Jesus; the altar is the shore of the eternal world and Jesus comes at the words of consecration. In the Holy Mass we know Him, yet our eyes are held from seeing Him. He is in another form. We cannot see him, but we know it is the Lord. Jesus prepares for us and gives us the Bread of Life. If we were to spend our whole lives in preparation, one such divine encounter would be an overpayment of all our prayer, penance, and purification of heart.

Yet Jesus comes to us, not once only, but morning by morning. Every day begins with Him! If the first hour of every day were spent in the presence—certain yet unseen—of our guardian angel or patron saint, our whole day would be elevated by it.

There is no fixed horizon to the multitude of His sweetness, which expands on every side like the limitless sea. And yet all its sweetness in hidden in the Blessed Sacrament for those who seek Him in holy reverence. Before Jesus departs from us for a season, to come again tomorrow, He takes and gives to us His precious Body and Blood as in the upper room, on that last night of farewell, and as at Emmaus, when He vanished from their sight. Jesus is gone, but in a little while He is to be found again, in the midst of His disciples. "He loved his own in the world and he loved them to the end" (John 13:1). Jesus left us a pledge of His love above the order and conditions of nature—His own perpetual Presence veiled from sight.

We are in contact with the eternal Word; and that contact is real and substantial and personal, both on His side and ours. We behold Him face to face by the vision of faith. Beyond there is nothing but the vision of the blessed. After the consecration we are already admitted to His vision, under a veil—we join the liturgy already taking place in heaven, surrounded by angels, saints, and martyrs in the heavenly court. From the consecration to the Communion we are as truly and more consciously with Christ than were Cleophas and his companion on the way to Emmaus. And though our eyes are held from seeing Him, our understanding is not. We see Him in another shape; but we know him while we see Him. And we speak to Him as our Lord, our Master, and our Friend; and by an inward speech He answers us in words which it is not in man to utter.

ACT OF HUMBLE CONFIDENCE

Dear Jesus, I come before You this day with hope, yet my hope is not in myself. I realize that I am like Your servant, Saint Paul, who said, "What I do, I do not understand. For I do not do what I want, but I do what I hate" (ROMANS 7:15).

O Lord, my hope is in You, for You have accepted me. In Baptism You made me a new creation, and You have given me power to become Your child. You are teaching me to surrender my fears, my pride, my selfishness, my lust, and my controlling attitudes, to You. In return, I receive Your peace, Your provision, Your guidance, and Your joy. I am Yours, O Lord, and Yours I wish to be, now and forever.

Your Word proclaims:

> My bones were not hidden from you,
> When I was being made in secret,
>   fashioned as in the depths of the earth.
> Your eyes foresaw my actions;
>   in your book all are written down;
>   my days were shaped, before one came to be.
>   —PSALM 139:15-16

Father, You knew me before I was born. You knew my strengths and weaknesses when You created me, and You understand me, O Lord. I receive You, now, into my heart. I receive Your acceptance of me, even though at this moment I may not feel accepted, or loved, or worthy of Your attention.

Dear God, like one who runs a race, help me when I stumble and fall, to rise again and press on to the goal You have set for me. Thank You that I don't have to reach anyone else's goal. You only call me to follow You; that is enough for me. I rejoice in Your faithful forgiveness always, should I fall, and I rely on Your unfailing grace to raise me up and set my feet upon a rock.

O Lord, You command us to rejoice always in You. You want your children to rejoice, even in trials, as a sign that we believe that You are always able to either deliver us from the trial or give us victory through it. Saint Paul reminds us, "Be content with what you have, for he has said, 'I will never forsake you or abandon you.' Thus we may say with confidence:

> 'The Lord is my helper,
> (and) I will not be afraid.
> What can anyone do to me?'"

—HEBREWS 13:5-6

Strengthened by Your Word today, I give myself and each person I meet, a fresh start, a new beginning. Forgetting what lies behind, I look up, to You, on this new day, and I am excited about what You are planning for me and all people. As I prepare to receive You in Holy Communion, I thank You for leaving heaven to save each of us and to give us everlasting life. You are awesome, Lord Jesus! To you belongs all the praise, all the glory, and all the love, with the Father and the Holy Spirit, now and forever. Amen!

ACT OF DESIRE

Thomas à Kempis

With the greatest devotion and burning love, and with all the affection and fervor of my heart, I desire to receive You, O Lord, as have many saints and devout persons, who were most pleasing to You in their holiness and fervent devotion. O God, my eternal love, my whole Good, my never-ending happiness, I long to receive You with the greatest desire and reverence which any of Your saints have ever felt or could feel. Although I am not worthy to have all these feelings of devotion, yet I offer to You all the affection of my heart, as if I alone had all those tender longings most pleasing to You. I desire to keep nothing for myself, but to freely and most willingly sacrifice myself and all that is mine to You.

O Lord my God, my Creator and my Redeemer, I desire to receive You this day with the same affection, love, gratitude, and faith, as did Your Holy Mother Mary, when she humbly answered the angel Gabriel. I offer You all the virtues and praises of all creatures in heaven and on earth, for myself and those for whom I wish to pray, that by all You may be worthily praised and glorified forever.

I invite and entreat the blessed in heaven and the faithful on earth to join with me in giving You praise and thanks. Let all people, nations, and languages praise You and magnify Your holy name with great jubilation and ardent devotion. Finally, dear Lord Jesus, let all who reverently and devoutly celebrate Your Most Holy Sacrament receive it with full faith, find grace and mercy at Your hands, and pray humbly for me a sinner. Amen.

AN ACT OF LOVE

Saint Augustine

By the shedding of Your precious Blood, through which we are redeemed, I beseech You, Lord Jesus, grant me heartfelt remorse and the gift of tears, particularly when I present to You my prayers and supplications, when I sing Your praise, when I assist at the celebration of the mysteries of our redemption, those pledges of Your love, and when I draw near to Your altar to receive this heavenly mystery with reverence and devotion.

O Lord, you gave us the Eucharist in commemoration of Your passion and death, and for the correction of our daily faults. May my soul be strengthened by Your presence in Holy Communion, may I feel You to be near and rejoice in You. O Jesus, everlasting and unchanging Light, Fire that ever burns, Light that shines perpetually, Bread of life on which we feed and which suffers no decrease; enlighten me, kindle me, and sanctify me. Deliver me from the evil one and fill me with Your grace that I may now eat Your flesh to the saving of my soul, and by this food, may I live in You, and rest forever in You.

I love You, O Good Jesus, with all the love of my heart, and by the help of Your grace I will love You ever and always. What shall I return to You, O Lord, for all You have given me? I surrender myself to You. Take possession of my heart, and rule in it as my only Lord and Master; count me as Your servant and do not permit me to set up any gods beside You, for You alone will I serve in life and in death. Amen.

BYZANTINE PRAYER
BEFORE COMMUNION

from the Divine Liturgy of Saint John Chrysostom

O Lord, I believe and profess that You are truly Christ, the Son of the Living God, Who came into the world to save sinners, of whom I am the first.

Accept me as a partaker of Your mystical supper, O Son of God, for I will not reveal Your mysteries to Your enemies, nor will I give you a kiss as did Judas, but like the thief I confess to You:

Remember me, O Lord, when You shall come into Your kingdom.

Remember me, O Master, when You shall come into Your kingdom.

Remember me, O Holy One, when You shall come into Your kingdom.

May the partaking of your holy mysteries, O Lord, be not for my judgment, or condemnation, but for the healing of soul and body.

O Lord, I also believe and profess that this, which I am about to receive, is truly Your most precious Body and Your life-giving Blood, which, I pray, make me worthy to receive for the remission of all my sins and for life everlasting. Amen.

O God, be merciful to me a sinner.

God, cleanse my sins and have mercy on me.

O Lord forgive me for I have sinned without number.

HUMILITY BEFORE THE LORD

Cardinal Newman

O my God, holiness befits Your house, and yet You make Your home in my heart. My Lord, My Savior, to me You come hidden under the semblance of earthly things, yet in that very flesh and blood which You took from Mary. You, who first inhabited Mary's breast, do now come to me. My God, You see me; I cannot see myself. Were I ever so good a judge about myself, ever so unbiased and with ever so correct a rule of judging, still, from my very nature, I cannot look at myself and view myself truly and wholly.

But You, as You come to me, contemplate me. When I say, "Lord, I am not worthy," You, whom I am addressing, alone understand in their fullness the words which I use. You see how unworthy so great a sinner is, to receive the One Holy God, whom the seraphim adore with trembling. You see not only the stains and scars of past sins, but also the mutilations, the deep cavities, and the chronic disorders they have left in my soul. You see the innumerable living sins, though they be not mortal, living in their power and presence, their guilt and their penalties which clothe me; You see all my bad habits, my insensitive attitudes, my wayward, lawless thoughts, my multitude of infirmities and miseries; yet You come. You see most perfectly how little I really feel what I am now saying, yet You come. O my God, left to myself should I not perish under the awful splendor and the consuming fire of Your Majesty? Enable me to bear You, lest I have to say with Peter: "Depart from me, for I am a sinful man, O Lord."

JESUS' DESIRE FOR US

"I have eagerly desired to eat this Passover with you
before I suffer."
—LUKE 22:15

Every single Mass in nothing more nor less than a renewal of
that great paroxysm of our Savior's passionate love for the soul;
another outbreak of that anguish which says, "with desire I have
desired." When shall we understand this or believe it? "He that
loves," says Thomas à Kempis, "knows the strong cry of the
lover."

Let us, if we have ever loved a child or mother or friend or
spouse, try and recall the hunger and thirst, the craving for
nearness and converse which love means, its restlessness and
burning energy. And let us add to all this whatever we have read

or heard of ardent, devoted passions. And let us cast all these longings into one love which holds in synthesis all that is best in each of them, and let us multiply its fervor seven times, and seven times again, until we see before us infinity stretching away beyond our utmost horizon; and then let us bring this infinite love and compress it into the finite compass of a human heart, bursting and breaking out under the strain of every side. Perhaps then we will have some dim notion of what goes on when day by day Christ Jesus comes hungering and thirsting for our love and breaks bread and says, "Take and eat, this is My Body which is given for you."

We can further hear Our Lord say, "Take all that I have, all that I am, make Me yours, dispose of me according to your good will and pleasure; do with Me what you like. I am your slave, at your mercy to use and abuse; crushed and humbled by hunger, ready for the very husks of the swine, the scraps and leavings of your love. Love I must have or perish. Give me all sort of love and this is enough for Me, though I would gladly have more. This is My Body that I gave to be torn into shreds for you, and would give a thousand times a day if necessary to be crucified again for you, the Body that I took for you, in hopes I might get you to love Me. And this is My Blood, My Heart's blood that I poured out for you and for all sinners that they might not come between us."

PRAYER TO THE BLESSED VIRGIN MARY

Mother of mercy and of love, most blessed Virgin Mary, I, a poor and unworthy sinner, fly to you with all my heart and all my affection. I implore your loving kindness, that even as you stood beside your dearly beloved Son as He hung upon the cross, so please also stand by me, a poor sinner; by the priest who is offering Mass here today; and beside all your faithful people receiving the most sacred Body of your Son. Through your intercession, may we offer a worthy and acceptable sacrifice in the sight of the most high and undivided Trinity, and receive Jesus in Holy Communion, worthily and fruitfully. Amen.

O Jesus, living in Mary,
Come and live in Your servants,
In the spirit of Your holiness,
In the fullness of Your might,
In the truth of your virtues,
In the perfection of your ways,
In the communion of Your mysteries;
Subdue every hostile power,
In Your spirit, for the glory of Your Father. Amen.

PRAYER TO SAINT JOSEPH

Saint Joseph, father and guardian of virgins, to whose faithful keeping Christ Jesus, innocence itself, and Mary, the virgin of virgins, were entrusted, I pray and beseech you by that twofold and most precious charge, by Jesus and Mary, to save me from all uncleanness, to keep my mind untainted, my heart pure, and my body chaste; and to help me always to serve Jesus and Mary in perfect chastity. Amen.

Prayer to Saint Joseph

Blessed Joseph, husband of Mary, be with us this day.
You protected and cherished the Virgin;
loving the Child Jesus as your Son,
you rescued him from danger of death.
Defend the Church, the household of God,
purchased by the blood of Christ.
Guardian of the holy family,
be with us in our trials.
May your prayers obtain for us
the strength to flee from error
and wrestle with the powers of corruption,
so that in life we may grow in holiness,
and in death rejoice in the crown of victory. Amen.

THANKSGIVING AFTER COMMUNION

You have just received Jesus in the Holy Eucharist—Jesus Himself! The Eternal Word who has no beginning nor end, the second person of the Blessed Trinity, the only Son of the Living God, the Son of Mary and of his chosen father Joseph: Your creator, Your redeemer, and Your best friend, whether you realize it or not. Praise God!

Under the species of bread, the Blessed Sacrament will remain in your body about 15 minutes before digestion. Enter into deep communion with Jesus, the one who knows you better and loves you more than anyone else does. Speak to Him; tell Him you love Him; let Him speak to you, in the quiet of your heart. Do not start reading at once, but be present to Him.

"My dear child, I love you. Nothing you could ever do could change My love for you. I understand you, for I created you. I have forgiven you all your sins. Be not afraid. I have come to save you. I am your Helper. I am your Protector. I am your Sun and your Shield. I am your Refuge. I am your strong Tower. Call unto Me, and I will answer you, and show you great and mighty things of which you do not know."

Let us take a few moments after Mass to just enjoy Jesus' presence and rest in His love. Let us thank Him from our hearts and tell Him we love Him. He knows we are weak and how easily we fall. Even so, He has redeemed us from sin and has given us eternal life. Eternal life is this intimate union with the Father and the Son in the Holy Spirit— communion with God and one another in the Body of Christ. Eternal life has come to us; eternal life is within us. Let us rejoice and be glad!

PRAYER AFTER COMMUNION

O Jesus, You have just come to me in Holy Communion.
Your Body is living in my body.
Your Heart is beating in my heart.
You are truly present in me now.
Thank You so much for coming into my heart!
I am so glad You are here with me.
Please don't ever leave me.
I love You, Jesus.
I want to live forever with You in heaven.
Today I give myself to You.
I give You my body, my mind, my heart.
Please keep me close to Your Heart,
and bring me back to You if ever I stray from You.
Jesus, I love You. Amen.

ANIMA CHRISTI
Soul of Christ

Soul of Christ, sanctify me;
Body of Christ, save me;
Blood of Christ, inebriate me;
Water from the side of Christ, wash me;
Passion of Christ, strengthen me;
O good Jesus, hear me;
Within Your wounds, hide me;
Separated from You, let me never be;
From the evil one, protect me;
At the hour of my death, call me;
And close to You, bid me;
That with Your saints, I may be,
Praising You forever and ever. Amen.

PRAYER OF SAINT THOMAS AQUINAS

Lord, Father all-powerful and ever-living God, I thank You, for even though I am a sinner, Your unprofitable servant, not because of my worth but in the kindness of Your mercy, You have fed me with the Precious Body and Blood of Your Son, our Lord Jesus Christ.

I pray that this Holy Communion may not bring me condemnation and punishment, but forgiveness and salvation. May it be a helmet of faith and a shield of good will. May it purify me from evil ways and put an end to my evil passions. May it bring me charity and patience, humility and obedience, and growth in the power to do good.

May it be my strong defense against all my enemies, visible and invisible, and the perfect calming of all my evil impulses, bodily and spiritual. May it unite me more closely to you, the One true God, and lead me safely through death to everlasting happiness with You.

And I pray that You will lead me, a sinner, to the banquet where You, with Your Son and Holy Spirit, are true and perfect light, total fulfillment, everlasting joy, gladness without end, and perfect happiness to Your saints. Grant this through Christ our Lord. Amen.

PRAYER OF SAINT BONAVENTURE

Saint Bonaventure, Franciscan, Bishop, and Doctor of the Church,
was one of the most beloved men of God in the Middle Ages.

Pierce, O most Sweet Lord Jesus, my inmost soul with the most joyous and healthful wound of Thy love, with true, serene, and most holy apostolic charity, that my soul may ever languish and melt with love and longing for Thee, that it may yearn for Thee and faint for Thy courts, and long to be dissolved and to be with Thee.

Grant that my soul may hunger after Thee, the bread of angels, the refreshment of holy souls, our daily and supersubstantial bread, having all sweetness and savor and every delight of taste; let my heart ever hunger after and feed upon Thee, upon whom the angels desire to look, and may my inmost soul be filled with the sweetness of Thy savor; may it ever thirst after Thee, the fountain of life, the fountain of wisdom and knowledge, the fountain of eternal light, the torrent of pleasure, the richness of the house of God.

May it ever compass Thee, seek Thee, find Thee, run to Thee, attain Thee, meditate upon Thee, speak of Thee, and do all things to the praise and glory of Thy name, with humility and discretion, with love and delight, with ease and affection, and with perseverance unto the end; may Thou alone be ever my hope, my entire assurance, my riches, my delight, my pleasure, my joy, my rest and tranquility, my peace, my sweetness, my fragrance, my sweet savor, my food, my refreshment, my refuge, my help, my wisdom, my portion, my possession and my treasure, in whom may my mind and my heart be fixed and firmly rooted immovably henceforth and for ever. Amen.

THE BREAD OF ANGELS

God had rained down manna upon them to eat,
and had given them the bread of heaven. Man ate the bread of angels.
—PSALM 77:24-25 (DOUAY RHEIMS BIBLE; cf. PSALM 78, NAB)

Angels' food is the food of the pure, for the pure shall see God, as clear water reflects the brilliance of the sun. The angels behold the face of God intuitively, by their very nature. Christ is the bread of angels; the angels feed their love with His presence. Christ satisfies their longing for truth, He who is Himself their truth and their life.

Christ is the bread of angels, the bread that makes us as angels, we who are so carnal, shortsighted, gross-minded, in every way unangelic! Here lies the mystery of Divine pity: Behold the bread of angels, made ready for our journey: true bread of children, not given to dogs. For as Jesus told the Syrophoenician woman who begged Him to heal her daughter: "Let the children be fed first. For it is not right to take the food of the children and throw it to the dogs" (MARK 7:27).

Yet what does God care about propriety and political correctness when the souls of sinners are in question? He has no sense of dignity or standoff self-respect, but He runs forward with all the weakness of passionate love, to meet us in our rags and filth, while we are yet a long way off; and He weeps, and kisses us, and clothes and crowns us, and banquets us, and goes on like one beside himself for ecstasy and joy. *Panis Angelicus, fit panis hominum*—Bread of Angels, made bread for men—come let me receive You in my heart today!

THE BENEFITS OF HOLY COMMUNION

The *Catechism of the Catholic Church* in paragraphs 1391-1398 lists the following fruits, or benefits, of Holy Communion:

- **Holy Communion increases our union with the Lord.** Remember Jesus' parable about the vine and the branches? A dead branch withers and dies apart from the vine. In like manner we need the Eucharist to keep us strong in Christ.

- **Holy Communion nourishes our spirits with all we need to grow spiritually.** It often imparts physical strength as well!

- **Holy Communion separates us from sin and its power.**

- **Holy Communion strengthens God's love within us.** It revives our hearts and empowers us to root ourselves in Christ.

- **Holy Communion preserves us from falling into mortal sin.** The closer we are to Christ, the harder it is for the enemy to pull us away from Him.

- **Holy Communion deepens our unity as Church.** The Eucharist actually makes the Church! Communion deepens our unity as the Body of Christ.

- **Holy Communion constrains us to recognize Christ in the poor and invites us to serve them.**

- **Holy Communion causes us to long for the full unity of all Christians and invites us to pray "that they may all be one"** (JOHN 17:21).

PRAYER OF SAINT IGNATIUS LOYOLA

Take O Lord, and receive all my liberty, my memory, my understanding, and my entire will. All that I am and all that I possess, You have given to me. I surrender it all to You; dispose of it according to Your will. Give me only Your love and Your grace, that's enough for me. With these I will be rich enough, and will desire nothing more. Amen.

THE EFFECTS OF FREQUENT COMMUNION
Mother Mary Loyola

Even after three years of close companionship with Jesus, the apostles noticed no striking change in each other, and little in themselves. Yet Jesus saw a steady transformation going forward, and He rejoiced. He saw how the love of Himself, which brings with it all good, was gradually raising their standards; was widening, purifying, and kindling their hearts; and preparing the material for fire which at Pentecost was to descend upon them and transform them into other men. Slowly and quietly, as is the way with the works of God, the apostles grew into the knowledge of the likeness of the Son of God, until each in his measure of capacity, and according to God's plan for him, became *alter Christus*—another Christ. So it will be with us.

PRAYER BEFORE A CRUCIFIX

Look down upon me, good
and gentle Jesus, while
before Your face I humbly
kneel and, with burning
soul, pray and beseech You
to fix deep in my heart
lively sentiments of faith,
hope, and charity;

true contrition for
my sins,

and a firm purpose of
amendment;

While I contemplate, with
great love and tender pity,

Your five most
precious wounds,

pondering over them within me
and calling to mind the words
which David, Your prophet,
said of You, my Jesus:

"They have pierced my hands and
my feet,

They numbered all my
bones."

Amen.

OUR TRUE PHYSICIAN

Based on a Meditation by Mother Loyola

As we read the accounts of Jesus' healings, we observe their number and their occurrence from personal contact with Jesus:

- He took the child by the hand and said to her, "Talitha koum," which means, "Little girl, I say to you, arise!" (MARK 5:41)
- But Jesus took him by the hand, raised him, and he stood up (MARK 9:27).
- Moved with pity, Jesus touched their eyes. Immediately they received their sight, and followed him (MATTHEW 20:34).
- And people brought to him a deaf man who had a speech impediment and begged him to lay his hand on him. [He took him off by himself away from the crowd. He put his finger into the man's ears and, spitting, touched his tongue; then he looked up to heaven and groaned, and said to him, "Ephphatha!" (that is, "Be opened!") And (immediately) the man's ears were opened, his speech impediment was removed, and he spoke plainly (MARK 7:32-35).

People knew that life and healing lay in Jesus' simple touch:

- An official came forward, knelt down before him, and said, "My daughter has just died. But come, lay your hand on her, and she will live" (MATTHEW 9:18).
- A woman suffering hemorrhages for twelve years came up behind him and touched the tassel on his cloak. She said to herself, "If only I can touch his cloak, I shall be cured." Jesus turned around and saw her, and said, "Courage, daughter! Your faith has saved you" (MATTHEW 9:20-22).

Note the repetition of the word "all" or "everyone" in reference to Our Lord's healings and cures:

- Everyone in the crowd sought to touch him because power came forth from him and healed them all (LUKE 6:19).
  His fame spread to all of Syria, and they brought to him all who were sick with various diseases and racked with pain, those who were possessed, lunatics, and paralytics, and he cured them (MATTHEW 4:24).
  At sunset, all who had people sick with various diseases brought them to him. He laid his hands on each of them and cured them (LUKE 4:40).

Dear Lord Jesus, to all those sorrowful and heavily burdened, You showed yourself more loyal than a brother. No sores were too loathsome for You to touch. Every sickness, no matter how terminal or chronic, had to yield to Your Word; all those with diseases were brought to You, and, by laying on Your hands, You healed every one of them.

And You, the same as then—are with me now, with the same, no, with greater compassion. You can see the wounds of my soul. I am too quick to believe that while the sicknesses of my body call for Your pity, You have only anger for the wounds of my soul. Yet, Your gentleness with sinners and Your tender handling of their brokenness gives me hope. Jesus, right now I cast myself at Your feet. I place myself beneath Your healing hand. I wait for the word that will heal, a little at a time, my pride, my coldness in prayer, my uncharitable tongue, my neglect of distasteful duties. Lord, if You will, You can heal me! Speak but the word, and I shall be healed! Amen.

PSALM 23

A psalm of David

The LORD is my shepherd;
    there is nothing I lack.
In green pastures you let me
        graze;
    to safe waters you lead me;
    you restore my strength.
You guide me along the right
        path
    for the sake of your name.

Even when I walk through a
        dark valley,
    I fear no harm for you are at
        my side;
    your rod and staff give me courage.

You set a table before me
    as my enemies watch;
You anoint my head with oil;
    my cup overflows.
Only goodness and love will pursue me
    all the days of my life;
I will dwell in the house of the LORD
        for years to come.

PSALM 121

A song of ascents

I raise my eyes toward the
    mountains.
  From where will my help
    come?
My help comes from the
    LORD,
  the maker of heaven and
    earth.

God will not allow your foot
    to slip;
  your guardian does not
    sleep.
Truly, the guardian of Israel
  never slumbers nor sleeps.
The LORD is your guardian;
  the LORD is your shade
  at your right hand.
By day the sun cannot harm
    you,
  nor the moon by night.
The LORD will guard you
    from all evil,
  will always guard your life.
The LORD will guard your coming and going
  both now and forever.

37

EUCHARISTIC DEVOTIONS

The heart of the Eucharist is its celebration in liturgy and its reception in Holy Communion. According to Vatican II, all legitimate devotions springing from the Eucharist, such as Exposition, Benediction, and Adoration, must flow from the celebration and lead to the reception of Holy Communion.

Benediction of the Blessed Sacrament is a blessing with the monstrance following some time of prayer and devotion before Our Lord present in the Blessed Sacrament. Adoration, or prayer before the Blessed Sacrament, includes the attitudes of adoration, thanksgiving, contrition, and petition. As such it is an extension of the spirit of prayer, which should fill the heart of Christians during the liturgy. Adoration also prepares us for the reception of Holy Communion by deepening our union with Christ in the Holy Spirit. An intimate union with Christ flows from such prayer.

Early in his papacy, Pope Saint John Paul II himself opened a chapel of Perpetual Eucharistic Adoration at Saint Peter's Basilica, signaling his great desire that the faithful renew their love for Eucharistic devotion. By his teaching, travels, and example, the Holy Father promoted a worldwide resurgence of such devotion.

"The worship given to the Trinity of the Father and of the Son and of the Holy Spirit ... must fill our churches. ... Adoration of Christ in this sacrament of love must also find expression in various forms of Eucharistic devotion: personal prayer before the Blessed Sacrament, hours of adoration, periods of exposition ... and Eucharistic benediction. ... Let us be generous with our time in going to meet him in adoration and in contemplation that is full of faith and ready to make reparation for the great faults and crimes of the world. May our adoration never cease." —POPE SAINT JOHN PAUL II

The Feast of Corpus Christi

Early in the 13th century, Our Lord revealed to Saint Juliana of Liege His desire for a feast to honor the Blessed Sacrament. Providentially, her obedience to Jesus' direction led to the establishment of the Feast of Corpus Christi—the Body of Christ—by Pope Urban IV in 1264. This feast provided, as it were, the foundation for worship of the Body of Christ in the Blessed Sacrament outside of the Mass itself, while at the same time providing the link between the liturgy and this devotion.

On the feast of Corpus Christi, the faithful would gather behind the priest holding the monstrance with the Blessed Sacrament under a festive canopy, and process together outside of the church into the fields and towns of medieval Europe. Acolytes and singers would lead the procession, while children would throw flowers along the path ahead of the Holy Eucharist. In our day many communities are returning to the custom of the Corpus Christ procession, hopefully more aware that Christ wants to be among His people in the world.

FORTY HOURS DEVOTION

*"Thus it is written that the Messiah would suffer and rise
from the dead on the third day."*

—LUKE 24:46

The Forty Hours Devotion is a special 40-hour period of prayer before the exposed Blessed Sacrament made by a community of the faithful. The devotion finds its roots in the 40 hours that Our Lord was in the tomb, from 3 PM Good Friday until 6 AM Easter Sunday. During that time, Mary and the apostles no doubt prayed, even in their suffering, and kept watch until the "third day" about which Jesus had spoken so often.

The actual Forty Hours devotion originated in Milan around 1530. Saints Philip Neri and Ignatius Loyola promoted this practice in the decades following, and in 1592, Pope Clement VIII established it in Rome.

In addition to nurturing our love for the Sacred Heart of Jesus in the Blessed Sacrament, the Forty Hours Devotion helps protect us from evil and temptation, offers us an opportunity to make reparation for our sins and those of the Poor Souls in Purgatory, and affords us deliverance from spiritual and physical calamities and difficulties.

In the Forty Hours Devotion, we are called to pray for ourselves and for our neighbors as well. We intercede for the needs of the world before the Lord of heaven and earth, and we wait upon Him. We adore the Blessed Sacrament "face to face." We console the Sacred Heart of Our Lord, and enter into spiritual communion with the Father, Son, and Holy Spirit.

PERPETUAL ADORATION

All of us, gazing with unveiled face on the glory of the Lord,
are being transformed into the same image from glory to glory,
as from the Lord who is the Spirit.

—2 CORINTHIANS 3:18

Perpetual Adoration is the uninterrupted adoration of Jesus Christ, present in the exposed Blessed Sacrament. Some churches today offer perpetual adoration, and many offer partial adoration for certain hours daily or regularly.

Exposition of the Blessed Sacrament and Perpetual Adoration began to grow as a devotion following the establishment of the feast of Corpus Christi, and later, the Forty Hours' Devotion. Today, during every hour of the day, every day of the year, Our Lord in the Blessed Sacrament is adored by the faithful throughout the world. Adoration enables us to thank Our Lord as we adore and praise Him for Who He is, what He has done, and what He continues to do for all people at all times.

Perpetual Adoration brings forth graces from heaven, leading to greater attendance at Mass, more frequent reception of the sacraments, especially Penance, an increase in conversions and vocations, the renewal of family life, a more fervent spirituality in the parish, and a more sincere love among the faithful. In a word, as we adore and love the Lord, He is transforming us into His image, to His honor and praise. We are becoming more holy and more human, for "the glory of God is man fully alive!"

BENEDICTION OF
THE BLESSED SACRAMENT

There are four elements of the rite of Benediction: Exposition, Adoration, Benediction, and Reposition. As the celebrant brings the Blessed Sacrament to the altar, you may sing the following hymn:

O Salutaris Hostia / O Saving Victim

O Salutaris Hostia
Quae coeli pandis ostium.
Bella premunt hostilia;
Da robur, fer auxilium.
Uni trinoque Domino
Sit sempiterna gloria:
Qui vitam sine termino,
Nobis donet in patria.
Amen.

—LATIN TEXT: SAINT THOMAS AQUINAS

O Saving Victim opening wide
The gate of heaven to all below.
Our foes press on from every side;
Thine aid supply, Thy strength bestow.
To Thy great name be endless praise
Immortal Godhead, One in Three;
Oh, grant us endless length of days,
In our true native land with Thee.
Amen.

—ENGLISH TEXT: EDWARD CASWALL

ADORATION

Our Lord Jesus in the Blessed Sacrament is exposed now on the altar. Together the assembly takes some time to worship the Lord silently and/or with appropriate prayers and hymns. The celebrant may give a brief homily at this time, to help us focus on Our Lord truly present, Body, Blood, Soul, and Divinity, in the Eucharist.

BENEDICTION

After some time of meditation, reflection, and contemplation, the celebrant prepares to bless the assembly. The following hymn is sung:

Tantum Ergo / Down in Adoration Falling

Tantum ergo sacramentum
Veneremur cernui:
Et antiquum documentum
Novo cedat ritui:
Praestet fides supplementum
Sensuum defectui.

Genitori, genitoque
Laus et iubilatio,
Salus, honor virtus quoque
Sit et benedictio:
Procedenti ab utroque
Compar sit laudatio. Amen.

—LATIN TEXT: SAINT THOMAS AQUINAS

Prayer Before the Eucharistic Blessing

Priest/Deacon: You have given them Bread from heaven (Alleluia).

ALL: Having all sweetness within it (Alleluia).

Priest/Deacon: Lord Jesus Christ, You gave us the Eucharist as the memorial of Your suffering and death. May our worship of this sacrament of Your Body and Blood help us to experience the salvation won for us and the peace of the kingdom, where You live with the Father and the Holy Spirit, one God, for ever and ever.

ALL: Amen.

The celebrant then takes the monstrance containing Our Lord and blesses all present. After blessing everyone, the priest reposes the Blessed Sacrament in the tabernacle.

The Divine Praises

Blessed be God.
Blessed be His Holy Name.
Blessed be Jesus Christ, true God and true man.
Blessed be the Name of Jesus.
Blessed be His Most Sacred Heart.
Blessed be His Most Precious Blood.
Blessed be Jesus in the Most Holy Sacrament of the Altar.
Blessed be the Holy Spirit, the Paraclete.
Blessed be the great Mother of God, Mary most holy.
Blessed be her holy and Immaculate Conception.
Blessed be her glorious Assumption.
Blessed be the name of Mary, Virgin and Mother.
Blessed be Saint Joseph, her most chaste spouse.
Blessed be God in His angels and in His Saints.

Holy God, We Praise Thy Name

TEXT: IGNAZ FRANZ
MELODY: TE DEUM

Holy God, we praise Thy name;
Lord of all, we bow before Thee;
All on earth Thy scepter claim;
All in heaven above adore Thee.
Infinite Thy vast domain;
Everlasting is thy reign!

Hark the loud celestial hymn;
Angel choirs above are raising;
Cherubim and seraphim,
In unceasing chorus praising;
Fill the heavens with sweet accord:
Holy, holy, holy Lord!

Holy Father, Holy Son,
Holy Spirit: three we name Thee;
Though in essence only one,
Undivided God we claim Thee;
And adoring bend the knee,
While we own the mystery.

ADORATION OF THE BLESSED SACRAMENT

Opening Prayer

My Lord Jesus Christ, it is Your great love for us that keeps You day and night in this Sacrament, full of pity and love, expecting inviting, and welcoming all who visit You. I believe that You are really present in the Sacrament of the Altar. From the depth of my nothingness, I adore You; and I thank You for the many graces You have given me, especially for the gift of Yourself in this Sacrament, for the gift of Your most holy Mother as my intercessor, and for the privilege of visiting You in this church.

I now speak to Your most loving Heart with a threefold intention: to thank You for the gift of Yourself; to atone for all the insults which Your enemies heap upon You in this Sacrament; and to adore You wherever Your Eucharistic Presence is dishonored or forgotten.

My Jesus, I love You with my whole heart. I am very sorry for my ingratitude to Your infinite goodness. I now resolve, with the help of Your grace, never to offend You again. And, sinful as I am, I consecrate to You my entire self, my whole will, my affections, my desires, and all that I have. From now on, do with me and mine as You please. I ask for and desire only Your love, final perseverance, and the grace always to do Your Holy Will.

I intercede with You for the souls in Purgatory, especially for those who were most devoted to the Blessed Sacrament, and to Your most holy Mother. I also recommend to You all poor sinners. And lastly, my dear Savior, I unite all my desires with the desires of Your most loving Heart. Thus united, I present them to Your Eternal Father and beg Him in Your Name and for the love of You to hear and answer them. Amen.

—SAINT ALPHONSUS LIGUORI

A VISIT TO THE BLESSED SACRAMENT

Saint Alphonsus Liguori

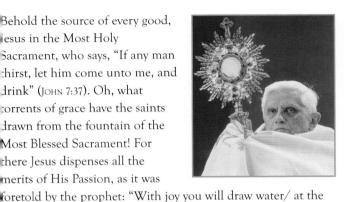

Behold the source of every good, Jesus in the Most Holy Sacrament, who says, "If any man thirst, let him come unto me, and drink" (JOHN 7:37). Oh, what torrents of grace have the saints drawn from the fountain of the Most Blessed Sacrament! For there Jesus dispenses all the merits of His Passion, as it was foretold by the prophet: "With joy you will draw water/ at the fountain of salvation" (ISAIAH 12:3). A holy woman, who loved to make long and frequent visits to Our Lord in the Blessed Sacrament, on being asked how she spent her many hours in the presence of the Holy of holies, answered: "I could remain there for all eternity. And is not there present the very essence of God, Who will be the food of the blessed? Good God! am I asked what I do in His presence? Why am I not rather asked, what is not done there? We love, we ask, we praise, we give thanks. We ask, what does a poor man do in the presence of one who is rich? What does a sick man do in the presence of his physician? What does a man do who is parched with thirst in the presence of a clear fountain? What is the occupation of one who is starving, and is placed before a splendid table?"

O my most amiable, most sweet, most beloved Jesus, my life, my hope, my treasure, the only love of my soul; oh, what has it cost You to remain thus with us in this Sacrament? You had to die, that You might thus dwell among us on our Altars; and then, how many insults have You not had to endure in this Sacrament, in order to aid us by Your Presence! Your love, and Your desire to be loved by us, have conquered all.

Come then, O Lord! Come and take possession of my heart; close its doors forever, that from now on no creature may enter there, to divide the love which is due to You, and which it is my ardent desire to bestow totally on You. I give You permission, my dear Redeemer, to rule me; to alone possess my whole being. If ever I do not obey You perfectly, chastise me with rigor, that from then on I may be more watchful to please You as You desire. Grant that I may no longer seek for any other pleasure than that of giving You pleasure; that all my pleasure may be to visit You often on Your altar; to entertain myself with You, and to receive You in Holy Communion. Let all who will, seek other treasures; the only treasure that I love, the only one that I desire, is that of Your love; for this only will I ask at the foot of the altar. Please make me forget myself, that thus I may only remember Your goodness. I envy you, blessed Seraphim, not for your glory, but for the love which you bear to our God; oh, please teach me what I must do to love Him and please Him.

My Jesus, I will love You only; You only do I desire to please. Amen.

SPIRITUAL COMMUNION

God loves you passionately! In his encyclical, *Deus Caritas Est*, Pope Benedict XVI describes God's desire for us as both erotic, seeking to receive our love, and agape, seeking to give us His love. Because He is God, His eros is also totally agape. The Cross proclaims this truth to all. Our God loves us so much and desires us so much to be with Him that He gave Himself for us in an eternal gift of true, selfless passion. He *is* love.

When we receive Jesus in sacramental Communion, we are truly one with God in a passionate embrace of love. However, we may experience this union with Him in spiritual Communion as well, when, in the words of Saint Thomas Aquinas, we have "an ardent desire to receive Jesus in the Most Holy Sacrament and to lovingly embrace Him." In spiritual Communion we humbly and contritely invite Jesus to come into our hearts as if we were receiving Him sacramentally. God gives us great graces in response to our desire to receive Him.

An Act of Spiritual Communion

My Jesus, I believe that You are truly present in the Blessed Sacrament. I love You above all things and I desire to receive You within my soul. Since I cannot now receive You sacramentally, come at least spiritually into my heart. *(Pause.)* I embrace You as being already there and unite myself wholly to You. Never permit me to be separated from You. Amen.

A VISIT TO OUR BLESSED MOTHER MARY

Saint Alphonsus loved Our Lady fervently, and he wrote the following prayer, urging everyone to visit Mary as part of their visit to Our Lord. Pray the following prayer to honor Our Lady and to obtain her most powerful patronage.

Most holy Immaculate Virgin and my Mother Mary, to you who are the Mother of my Lord, the Queen of the world, the advocate, the hope, and the refuge of sinners, I have recourse today—I, who am the most miserable of all. I render you my most humble homage, O Great Queen, and I thank you for all the graces you have conferred on me until now, particularly for having delivered me from hell, which I have so often deserved.

I love you, O most amiable Lady; and for the love which I bear you, I promise to serve you always, and to do all in my power to make others love you also. I place in you all my hopes; I confide my salvation to your care. Accept me for your servant, and receive me under your mantle, O Mother of mercy. And since you are so powerful with God, deliver me from all temptations, or rather obtain for me the strength to triumph over them until death. Of you I ask a perfect love for Jesus Christ. From you I hope to die a good death. O my Mother, by the love which you have for God, I beseech you to help me at all times, but especially at the last moment of my life. Leave me not, I beg you, until you see me safe in heaven, blessing you, and singing your mercies for all eternity. Amen. So I hope. So may it be.

CLOSING PRAYER
TO THE BLESSED SACRAMENT

As this time of Love closes, O Jesus, I renew my faith and trust in You. I am refreshed after my visit with You and I count myself among a privileged number, even as Your disciples were, who shared Your actual presence.

Realizing that my visit to You is of little help unless I try to live a better life and set a better example, I am resolved to go forth again to my duties and concerns with a renewed spirit of perseverance and good will. In my daily life I will try to love and serve God well, and love my neighbor also, for those two things go together. I will try to be a true disciple indeed. Help me, dear Jesus, in this my resolution.

Bless me, dear Lord, before I go. And bless not me alone, O Lord, but all who are here present as well, and all who could not come, especially the sick and the dying. Bless our homes and everyone there. Bless all our lives and the hour of our death.

Grant rest to the souls of the faithful departed, and bring them into the light of Your divine glory. So may we who have worshipped You and been blessed by You here on earth come to behold the radiant glory of Your unveiled countenance in heaven forever and ever. Amen.

Final Prayer

O, Sweet Jesus, let me lay at Your sacred feet my daily share of joys, struggles, and sorrows, of hopes, fears, and failings. Gather them tenderly into Your most Sacred Heart. Solace my doubts and calm my fears. Grant that I may become more united to You. Amen.

MULTIPLICATION

By Alfred Joyce Kilmer

I take my leave, with sorrow, of Him I love so well;
I look my last upon His small and radiant prison-cell;
O happy lamp! to serve Him with never ceasing light!
O happy flame! to tremble forever in His sight!

I leave the holy quiet for the loudly human train,
And my heart that He has breathed upon is filled with lonely
pain.
O King, O Friend, O Lover! What sorer grief can be
In all the reddest depths of Hell than banishment from Thee?

But from my window as I speed across the sleeping land
I see the towns and villages wherein His houses stand.
Above the roofs I see a cross outlined against the night,
And I know that there my Lover dwells in His sacramental
might.

Dominions kneel before Him, and Powers kiss His feet,
Yet for me He keeps His weary watch in the turmoil of the
street:
The King of Kings awaits me, wherever I may go,
O who am I that He should deign to love and serve me so?

Joyce Kilmer (1886-1918) was an American journalist and poet best known for
his poem, _Trees_. He was killed by a sniper at the end of World War I in
France, where he is buried.

HOLY HOUR DEVOTIONS

Psalm 51

Have mercy on me, God, in your
goodness;
    in your abundant compassion
    blot out my offense.
Wash away all my guilt;
    from my sin cleanse me.
For I know my offense;
    my sin is always before me.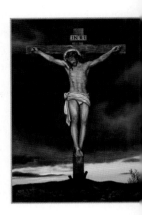
Against you alone have I sinned;
    I have done such evil in your
    sight
That you are just in your sentence,
    blameless when you condemn.
True, I was born guilty,
    a sinner, even as my mother conceived me.
Still, you insist on sincerity of heart;
    in my inmost being teach me wisdom.
Cleanse me with hyssop, that I may be pure;
    wash me, make me whiter than snow.
Let me hear sounds of joy and gladness;
    let the bones you have crushed rejoice.
Turn away your face from my sins;
    blot out all my guilt.
A clean heart create for me, God;
    renew in me a steadfast spirit.

Do not drive me from your presence,
    nor take from me your holy spirit.
Restore my joy in your salvation;
    sustain in me a willing spirit.
I will teach the wicked your ways,
    that sinners may return to you.
Rescue me from death, God, my saving God,
    that my tongue may praise your healing power.
Lord, open my lips;
    my mouth will proclaim your praise.
For you do not desire sacrifice;
    a burnt offering you would not accept.
My sacrifice, God, is a broken spirit;
    God, do not spurn a broken, humbled heart.

Make Zion prosper in your good pleasure;
    rebuild the walls of Jerusalem.
Then you will be pleased with proper sacrifice,
    burnt offerings and holocausts;
    then bullocks will be offered on your altar.

An Act of Adoration

We adore Thee, most holy Lord Jesus Christ, here and in all
Thy churches that are in the whole world, and we bless Thee,
because by Thy Holy Cross Thou hast redeemed the world.

—SAINT FRANCIS OF ASSISI

PETITIONS OF LOVE

By Saint Augustine

Lord Jesus, let me know myself and know Thee,
And desire nothing else but only Thee.
Let me hate myself and love Thee.
Let me do everything for the sake of Thee.

Let me humble myself and exalt Thee.
Let me think of nothing except Thee.
Let me die to myself and live in Thee.
Let me accept whatever happens as from Thee.

Let me banish self and follow Thee,
And ever desire to follow Thee.
Let me fly from myself and take refuge in Thee,
That I may deserve to be defended by Thee.

Let me fear for myself, let me fear Thee,
And let me be among those who are chosen by Thee.
Let me distrust myself and put my trust in Thee.
Let me be willing to obey for the sake of Thee.

Let me cling to nothing but only to Thee,
And let me be poor because of Thee.
Look upon me, that I may love Thee.
Call me, that I may see Thee,
And forever enjoy Thee. Amen.

PRAYER OF ADMIRATION

Who could have imagined, dearest Jesus, that You would love us so dearly? Was it not sufficient evidence of Your boundless affection to have left Your throne in heaven, where countless angels adored, to become man, and thus, God and Man, to live in the midst of us, as one of the poorest and most destitute?

Was this not proof abundant to convince the most skeptical that Your delight is to be with the children of men?

Yet most marvelous to us of all, is that even though You, truly God and Man, lived among us, yet this could not satisfy Your fathomless and incomprehensible love. It demanded a union far more intimate. Therefore You devised what could never be numbered among the conceptions of the human heart, and You, the Second Person of the Blessed Trinity, Jesus, the Son of Mary, became for us the Bread of Life! Yes, most loving Jesus, You enter our bodies and descend into our hearts, where a union more wonderful than any imagined is accomplished.

When You took little children in your arms to bless them, when Saint John rested on You at the Last Supper, when You rested and slept on Your mother's lap, close were these unions. But dearer, closer than all, is that union which takes place in Holy Communion. You become one with us and we with You, like two pieces of wax that are melted and joined together. We and our Beloved are one—so intimate that it is as though Your heart beat in our chest, and Your blood circulated in our veins. In this rapture, we may now exclaim, "I live, no longer I, but Christ lives in me" (GALATIANS 2:20). Thank You, dear Jesus, thank You, thank You, thank You!

THE FOOD OF THE SOUL
"FOR YOU MY SOUL HATH THIRSTED"

Cardinal Newman

In You, O Lord, all things live, and You give them their food. *Oculi omnium in Te sperant*—"the eyes of all hope in You." To the beasts of the field You give food and drink. They live on day by day, because You give them day by day to live. And, if You do not give, they feel their misery at once. Nature witnesses to this great truth, for they are visited at once with great agony, and they cry out and wildly wander about, seeking what they need. But, as to us Your children, You feed us with another food. You know, O my God who made us, that nothing can satisfy us but Yourself, and therefore You have caused Your own self to be food and drink for us. O most adorable mystery! O most stupendous of mercies!

You most Glorious, and Beautiful, and Strong, and Sweet; You knew well that nothing else would support our immortal natures, our frail hearts, but Yourself; and so You took on human flesh and blood, that they, as being the flesh and blood of God, might be our life.

O what an awesome thought! You deal otherwise with others, but, as to me, the flesh and blood of God is my sole life. I shall perish without it; yet shall I not perish with it and by it? How can I raise myself to such an act as to feed upon God? O my God, I am in a quandary—shall I go forward, or shall I go back?

I will go forward: I will go to meet You. I will open my mouth, and receive Your gift. I do so with great awe and fear, but what else can I do? To whom should I go but to You? Who can save me but You? Who can cleanse me but You? Who can make me overcome myself but You? Who can raise my body from the grave but You? Therefore I come to You in all these my necessities: in fear, but in faith.

My God, You are my life; if I leave You, I cannot but thirst. Lost spirits thirst in hell, because they have not God. They thirst, though they would have it otherwise, from the necessity of their original nature. But I, my God, wish to thirst for You with a better thirst. I wish to be clad in that new nature, which so longs for You from loving You, as to overcome in me the fear of coming to You. I come to You, O Lord, not only because I am unhappy without You, not only because I feel I need You, but because Your grace draws me on to seek You for Your own sake, because You are so glorious and beautiful.

I come in great fear, but in greater love. O may I never lose, as years pass away, and the heart shuts up, and all things are a burden, let me never lose this youthful, eager, elastic love of You. Make Your grace supply the failure of nature. Do the more for me, the less I can do for myself. The more I refuse to open my heart to You, so much the fuller and stronger be Your supernatural visitations, and the more urgent and efficacious Your presence in me. Amen.

A CONVERSATION WITH JESUS

Jesus: "O My child, if you only knew the power you have over My Heart, you would do it a holy violence; you would wrest from me the holy grace that the violent bear away. You would save sinners who are going to refuse their last grace. You would rescue the little children whose parents have given them over to be slain. You would place at once in heaven the souls that are crying for your pity and your help. You would strengthen the hands and cheer the hearts of My dearly beloved missionaries who carry My name to those who know Me not.

"You would win the light of faith for those who are seeking it, and strength for those who have found the treasure but lack the courage to sell all they have to purchase it. If you knew what I have done for you in giving you Myself, if you had faith as a grain of mustard seed, you would stretch forth your hand to strong things, and the fruits of your Communion would reach to the uttermost parts of the earth, into the dreary land of Purgatory, where redeemed souls are to be saved and helped."

Myself: "I wish, O Lord, that I could open Your way into every heart, that I could put the keys of every fortress over the wide earth into Your hands. But they are already there. Not only the keys of death and hell, but also the key to every human heart is in Your keeping. You know all its complex chambers; the rust of years that makes access difficult is no bar to You. Every difficulty yields to Your touch. You hold the key O Lord; rather, You Yourself *are* the key: 'The holy one, the true, / who holds the key of David, / who opens and no one shall close, / who closes and no one shall open'" (REVELATIONS 3:7).

PRAYER OF THANKSGIVING

O Lord, how can I thank You for giving Yourself to me? I am so needy, I can be so selfish, so empty, so unconcerned about You or others, yet You give yourself totally to me. Nothing I can do could ever change Your love for me. Nothing. That does not give me a license to sin, for as I sow, so shall I reap. Even so, the truth of Your unchanging, unconditional love for me brings me peace and a serene hope. I am worth saving. You died for me, and as You said, no one can take me out of your Father's hands. Praise God!

Faith reveals to me that in Holy Communion I receive benefits which the human heart cannot comprehend. I desired greatly to receive You and behold—You are here with me now. I longed for You, and You have come to me. With David I say, "Return, my soul, to your rest; / the LORD has been good to you" (PSALM 116:7).

O my soul, glorify the Lord your God! Acknowledge His goodness, extol His magnificence, and eternally proclaim His mercy! You flowers, lend me your perfumes; you trees, bend down your tops; you mountains, burn like holocausts. O that I could convert the entire universe into one temple and fill it with my voice to celebrate the praises of my God and Savior! Dear Mary, mother of God, lend me your heart with which to love Him; You blessed angels, lend me your fervor; all you saints, come to my aid. O Lord, I unite myself to every creature in heaven and on earth, and exclaim, "Salvation comes from our God, who is seated on the throne, / and from the Lamb. ... Blessing and glory, wisdom and thanksgiving, / honor, power, and might / be to our God forever and ever. Amen" (REVELATIONS 7:10, 12).

PRAYER OF HUMILITY

O Gift of gifts, O gracious call,
My God, how can it be,
That You who have discerning love,
Should give that gift to me?

How many hearts You might have
had,
More innocent than mine;
How many souls more worthy far,
Of that sweet touch of Thine?

O Grace! Unto unlikeliest hearts
It is Thy boast to come.
The glory of Thy light to find
In darkest spots a home.

Thy choice, O God of goodness! Then
I lovingly adore;
O give me grace to keep Thy grace,
And grace to merit more.

PRAYER OF DESIRE

As the deer longs for running waters, so Lord Jesus, my Redeemer, my soul longs for You, desiring to receive You, and to draw waters with joy out of Your fountains. Grown weary of walking in evil ways, I come to my deliverer crying to You, "Son of David have mercy on me, and give me the bread which shall revive me!"

Would that I could awaken within my soul the eager burning desire of the saints, that I may long without ceasing for You, the fount of life, of wisdom, and of never-ending joy. Would that I could hunger continually for You, You bread of life and refreshment for devout souls, and experience Your sweetness in my inmost heart.

My soul can know no consolation until I find You, O sovereign Lord, whom I desire most fervently, with the earnestness and reverence of all just men and saints, whose merits I offer to You in compensation for my shortcomings. Lord Jesus, may You alone be my delight, my peace, my strength, and my riches, in whom my soul can rest. I long for nothing beside You; in nothing else but You do I take pleasure, O God, the chief desire of my heart. O Jesus, Fount of charity, that flame which consumes all my sins, hide us in Your dear heart, that we may derive grace to love You here and possess You hereafter, who are our sole and supreme happiness. With the Father and the Holy Spirit, You are highly extolled forever, Lord Jesus. Amen.

JESUS, INCARNATE WISDOM

*But if any of you lacks wisdom, he should ask God who gives to all
generously and ungrudgingly, and he will be given it.*
—JAMES 1:5

Wisdom is the perfect knowledge of and the perfect adherence
to good in its essence. The soul that possesses wisdom,
contemplates its perfection, and tastes its sweetness, is
penetrated with God's holiness. The saints never tired of prayer
because they found in it the joy which God communicates to
generous souls who possess that supernatural wisdom
conquered by their generous constancy. I, too, desire this
wisdom, which, like a living flame, enkindles fervent love, and
warms the heart in such a way that all the powers of the soul
unite themselves, in an ineffable way, to God. I wish for this
wisdom, which makes the soul constant in the practice of
virtue, because it no longer loses the divine presence, which is
its light and support. I long for this wisdom but who will give it
to me? Only Jesus Himself.

Jesus, Incarnate Wisdom, whom I have loved and sought from
my youth, and have desired to take for my spouse, and of whose
beauty I became a lover, comes to me, the poorest and most
wretched soul, perhaps, of all those who have recourse to Him.
I did not recognize the value of the supernatural gifts of grace; I
neither sought nor longed for them; yet now, penitent, I do
seek and long for them. I am resolved to prefer heavenly
treasures to earthly ones, to grieve over those neglected in the
past, and to beg for divine wisdom.

esus comes to grant this prayer by giving Himself up entirely in n interior embrace of my heart, drawing to Himself all my ffections which heretofore wandered on earth, in order to raise hem to His Father in heaven. Jesus, the Eternal Wisdom, ishes to sanctify and make holy, by His divine contact, the emple of my soul.

Jesus, I long for You, of whom it is said, "He who watches for er at dawn shall not be disappointed, / for he shall find her itting by his gate" (WISDOM 6:14). In Your Word it is written, Those who love me I also love, / and those who seek me find e" (PROVERBS 8:17). You clearly tell us, "Behold, I stand at the oor and knock. If anyone hears my voice and opens the door, hen) I will enter his house and dine with him, and he with e" (REVELATIONS 3:20).

Jesus, I adore You. Please come into my heart, my soul, and y spirit. Take possession of me. To You alone belongs the ingdom of my powers. Direct them; fill my memory that it may hink constantly of You, my intellect that it may know Your ivine perfections, and my will that it may be more moved by ou to achieve good. I do not deserve this grace, but I hope for from Your mercy. My heart, like a hard stone, will melt with ove for You if You will grant me this wisdom and make me row in it. O Lord, abide with me. Be the sun that never sets, hat I may remain steadfast in the way of the Lord.

Mary, seat of wisdom, grant me your mighty assistance, "For here is nought God loves, be it not one who dwells with Wisdom" (WISDOM 7:28).

EUCHARISTIC ASPIRATIONS

Eternal Father! I offer You the precious blood of Jesus in satisfaction for my sins and for the wants of Your Holy Church. (Pope Pius VII)

O Jesus in the most holy Sacrament, have mercy on us. (Saint Pius X)

O Jesus I adore You here present in the Sacrament of your love. (Saint Pius IX)

O Jesus Christ, Son of the living God, Light of the World, I adore you; for You I live, for You I die. (Saint Pius X)

Our Lady of the most Blessed Sacrament, pray for us. (Saint Pius X)

Sing praise to God, sing praise;
sing praise to our king, sing praise.
-Psalm 47:6

"Yes, so mighty is God,
our God who leads us always!"
—Psalm 48:14

Offer praise as your sacrifice to God;
fulfill your vows to the Most High.
—Psalm 50:14

"My soul proclaims the greatness of the Lord;
my spirit rejoices in God my savior."
—Luke 1:46-47

"Behold our God, to whom we looked to save us!
This is the LORD for whom we looked;
let us rejoice and be glad that he has saved us!"
—ISAIAH 25:9

O LORD, our Lord,
how awesome is your name through all the earth!
You have set your majesty above the heavens!
—PSALM 8:1

have found Him whom my soul loves; I hold Him, and will
not let Him go. I embrace You, dear Jesus, and receive the full
joy of my love. I possess You, the treasure of my heart, in whom
possess all things. I implore You, let my soul feel the power of
our presence; let it taste how sweet You are, O my Lord, that
ed captive by Your love, it may seek no one else besides You,
nor love anyone else but for Your sake.

You are my King, forget not my tribulation and my need. You
re my Judge; spare me, and be merciful to me a sinner. You are
my Physician; heal all my infirmities. You are the spouse of my
oul; betroth me to Yourself forevermore. You are my Leader
nd my Defender; place me by Your side, and then I do not care
who lifts his hand against me. You have offered your self a
Victim for me, and I will offer to You a sacrifice of praise.

You are my Redeemer; redeem my soul from the power of hell
nd preserve me. You are my God and my all; for whom have I
n heaven but You, and besides You what do I desire or need?
You, my God, are the God of my heart and my portion forever.
Amen.

LITANY OF THE PRECIOUS BLOOD OF JESUS

Lord, have mercy. Lord, have mercy.
Christ, have mercy. Christ have mercy.
Lord, have mercy. Lord, have mercy.
Jesus hear us. Jesus, graciously hear us.
God the Father of Heaven, R. Have mercy on us.
God the Son, Redeemer of the world,
God the Holy Spirit,
Holy Trinity, One God,
Blood of Christ, only-begotten Son of the eternal Father,
R. Save us.
Blood of Christ, Incarnate Word of God,
Blood of Christ, of the New and Eternal Testament,
Blood of Christ, falling upon the earth in the Agony,
Blood of Christ, shed profusely in the Scourging,
Blood of Christ, flowing forth in the Crowning with Thorns,
Blood of Christ, poured out on the Cross,
Blood of Christ, Price of our salvation,
Blood of Christ, without which there is no forgiveness,
Blood of Christ, Eucharistic drink and refreshment of souls,
Blood of Christ, stream of mercy,
Blood of Christ, Victor over demons,
Blood of Christ, courage of Martyrs,
Blood of Christ, strength of Confessors,
Blood of Christ, bringing forth Virgins,
Blood of Christ, help of those in peril,
Blood of Christ, relief of the burdened,

Blood of Christ, solace in sorrow, R. Save us.
Blood of Christ, hope of the penitent,
Blood of Christ, consolation of the dying,
Blood of Christ, peace and tenderness of hearts,
Blood of Christ, pledge of eternal life,
Blood of Christ, freeing souls from purgatory,
Blood of Christ, most worthy of all glory and honor,

Lamb of God, Who takes away the sins of the world,
Spare us, O Lord.
Lamb of God, Who takes away the sins of the world,
Graciously hear us, O Lord.
Lamb of God, Who takes away the sins of the world,
Have mercy on us.
V. Thou has redeemed us, O Lord, in Thy Blood.
R. And made of us a kingdom for our God.

Let us pray: Almighty and eternal God,
You have appointed Your only-begotten Son
the Redeemer of the world
and willed to be appeased by His Blood.
Grant, we beg of You,
that we may worthily adore
this price of our salvation,
and through its power
be safeguarded from the evils of the present life,
so that we may rejoice
in its fruits forever in heaven.
Through the same Christ our Lord. Amen.

LITANY OF THE HOLY NAME OF JESUS

Lord, have mercy on us. Christ, have mercy on us.

Lord, have mercy on us. Jesus, hear us. Jesus, graciously hear us.

God the Father of Heaven, R. Have mercy on us.

God the Son, Redeemer of the world,

God the Holy Spirit,

Holy Trinity, One God,

Jesus, Son of the living God,

Jesus, Splendor of the Father,

Jesus, Brightness of eternal light,

Jesus, King of glory,

Jesus, Sun of justice,

Jesus, Son of the Virgin Mary,

Jesus, most amiable,

Jesus, most admirable,

Jesus, the mighty God,

Jesus, Father of the world to come,

Jesus, Angel of great counsel,

Jesus, most powerful,

Jesus, most patient,

Jesus, most obedient,

Jesus, meek and humble of heart,

Jesus, Lover of chastity,

Jesus, our Lover,

Jesus, God of peace,

Jesus, Author of life,

Jesus, Model of virtues,

Jesus, zealous for souls,

Jesus, our God, R. Have mercy on us.

Jesus, our Refuge,

Jesus, Father of the poor,

Jesus, Treasure of the faithful,

Jesus, Good Shepherd,

Jesus, true Light,

Jesus, eternal Wisdom,

Jesus, infinite Goodness,

Jesus, our Way and our Life,

Jesus, Joy of the Angels,

Jesus, King of Patriarchs,

Jesus, Master of the Apostles,

Jesus, Teacher of the Evangelists,

Jesus, Strength of Martyrs,

Jesus, Light of Confessors,

Jesus, Purity of Virgins,

Jesus, Crown of all Saints,

Be merciful, Spare us, O Jesus.

Be merciful, Graciously hear us, O Jesus!

From all evil, R. Jesus, deliver us.

From all sin,

From Your wrath,

From the snares of the devil,

From the spirit of fornication,

From everlasting death,

From the neglect of Your inspirations,

Through the mystery of Your Holy Incarnation,

Through Your Nativity,

Through Your Infancy,

Through Your most divine Life, R. Jesus, deliver us.
Through Your labors,
Through Your Agony and Passion,
Through Your Cross and dereliction,
Through Your Sufferings,
Through Your Death and Burial,
Through Your Resurrection,
Through Your Ascension,
Through Your Institution of the Most Holy Eucharist,
Through Your joys,
Through Your glory,
Lamb of God, Who takes away the sins of the world,
Spare us, O Jesus!
Lamb of God, Who takes away the sins of the world,
Graciously hear us, O Jesus!
Lamb of God, Who takes away the sins of the world,
Have mercy on us, O Jesus!
Jesus, hear us. Jesus, graciously hear us.

Let us pray: Lord Jesus Christ, You have said, "Ask and you shall receive; seek and you shall find; knock and it shall be opened to you." Mercifully attend to our supplications, and grant us the grace of Your most divine love, that we may love You with all our hearts, and in all our words and actions, and never cease to praise You. Grant us, O Lord, to have a perpetual awe and love of Your holy name, for You never fail to govern those whom You establish in Your love. We ask this of You, Who lives and reigns with Your Father and the Holy Spirit, One God, forever and ever. Amen.

LITANY OF THE BLESSED SACRAMENT

Saint Peter Julian Eymard

Lord, have mercy. Lord, have mercy.

Christ, have mercy. Christ, have mercy.

Lord, have mercy. Lord, have mercy.

Christ hear us. Christ graciously hear us.

God the Father of heaven, R. Have mercy on us.

God the Son, Redeemer of the world,

God the Holy Spirit,

Holy Trinity, one God,

Jesus, Eternal High Priest of the Eucharistic Sacrifice,

Jesus, Divine Victim on the altar for our salvation,

Jesus, hidden under the appearance of bread,

Jesus, dwelling in the tabernacles of the world,

Jesus, really, truly, and substantially present in the Blessed Sacrament,

Jesus, abiding in Your fullness, Body, Blood, Soul, and Divinity,

Jesus, Bread of Life,

Jesus, Bread of Angels,

Jesus, with us always until the end of the world,

Sacred Host, summit and source of all worship and Christian life, R. Have mercy on us.
Sacred Host, sign and cause of the unity of the Church,
Sacred Host, adored by countless angels,
Sacred Host, spiritual food,
Sacred Host, Sacrament of love,
Sacred Host, bond of charity,
Sacred Host, greatest aid to holiness,
Sacred Host, gift and glory of the priesthood,
Sacred Host, in which we partake of Christ,
Sacred Host, in which the soul is filled with grace,
Sacred Host, in which we are given a pledge of future glory,

Blessed be Jesus in the Most Holy Sacrament of the Altar.
Blessed be Jesus in the Most Holy Sacrament of the Altar.
Blessed be Jesus in the Most Holy Sacrament of the Altar.

For those who do not believe in Your Eucharistic presence, R. have mercy, O Lord.
For those who are indifferent to the Sacrament of Your love,
For those who have offended You in the Holy Sacrament of the Altar,

That we may show fitting reverence when entering Your holy temple, R. We beseech You, hear us.
That we may make suitable preparation before approaching the altar,
That we may receive You frequently in Holy Communion with real devotion and true humility,

That we may never neglect to thank You for so wonderful a
blessing, R. We beseech You, hear us.

That we may cherish time spent in silent prayer before You,

That we may grow in knowledge of this Sacrament of
sacraments,

That all priests may have a profound love of the Holy Eucharist,

That they may celebrate the Holy Sacrifice of the Mass in
accordance with its sublime dignity,

That we may be comforted and sanctified with Holy Viaticum
at the hour of our death,

That we may see You one day face to face in Heaven,

Lamb of God, Who takes away the sins of the world,
Spare us, O Lord!

Lamb of God, Who takes away the sins of the world,
Graciously hear us, O Lord!

Lamb of God, Who takes away the sins of the world,
Have mercy on us!

V. O Sacrament Most Holy, O Sacrament Divine,

R. All praise and all thanksgiving, be every moment Thine.

Let us pray:

Most merciful Father, You continue to draw us to Yourself
through the Eucharistic Mystery. Grant us fervent faith in this
Sacrament of love, in which Christ the Lord Himself is
contained, offered, and received. We make this prayer through
the same Christ our Lord. Amen.

LITANY FOR HOLY COMMUNION

Lord, have mercy on us. Christ, have mercy on us.
Lord, have mercy on us.
Christ, hear us. Christ graciously hear us.
God the Father of Heaven, R. Have mercy on us.
God the Son, Redeemer of the world,
God the Holy Spirit,
Holy Trinity, One God,
Jesus, living Bread which came down from Heaven,
Jesus, Bread from Heaven giving life to the world,
Jesus, hidden God and Savior,
Jesus, Who has loved us with an everlasting love,
Jesus, Whose delight is to be with the children of men,
Jesus, Who has given Your Flesh for the life of the world,
Jesus, Who invites all to come to You,
Jesus, Who promises eternal life to those who receive You,
Jesus, Who with desire desires to eat this Pasch with us,
Jesus, ever ready to receive and welcome us,
Jesus, Who stands at our door knocking,
Jesus, Who receives us into Your arms and blesses us with the
little children,
Jesus, Who invites us to lean on Your bosom with the beloved
disciple,
Jesus, Who has not left us orphans,
Most dear Sacrament,
Sacrament of love,
Sacrament of sweetness,
Life-giving Sacrament,

acrament of strength, R. Have mercy on us.

Ay God and my all,

'hat our hearts may pant after You as the deer after the
ountains of water, R. We beseech You, hear us.

'hat we may know Your voice as did Mary Magdalen,

'hat with a lively faith we may confess with the beloved
isciple, "It is the Lord!"

'hat You would bless us who have not seen, yet have believed,

'hat we may love You in the Blessed Sacrament with our whole
eart, our whole soul, all our mind, and with all our strength,

'hat the fruit of each Communion may be fresh love,

'hat our one desire may be to love You and to do Your will,

'hat we may ever remain in Your love,

'hat You would teach us how to receive and welcome You,

'hat You would teach us to pray, and pray within us,

'hat with You every virtue may come into our souls,

'hat throughout this day You would keep us closely united to
'ou,

'hat You would give us grace to persevere to the end,

'hat You would then be our support and Viaticum,

'hat with You and leaning on You we may safely pass through
ll dangers,

'hat our last act may be one of perfect love and our last breath
long deep sigh to be in Our Father's house,

'hat Your sweet face may smile upon us when we appear before
'ou,

'hat our banishment from You, dearest Lord, may not be very
ong,

That when the time is come, we may fly up from our prison to You, and in Your Sacred Heart find our rest forever,
R. We beseech You, hear us.
Lamb of God, Who takes away the sins of the world,
Spare us, O Lord!
Lamb of God, Who takes away the sins of the world,
Graciously hear us, O Lord!
Lamb of God, Who takes away the sins of the world,
Have mercy on us!

V. Stay with us, Lord, because it is toward evening,
R. And the day is now far spent.

Let us pray:
We come to You, dear Lord, with the Apostles, saying, "Increase our faith." Give us a strong and lively faith in the mystery of Your Real Presence in the midst of us. Give us the splendid faith of the centurion, which drew from You such praise. Give us the faith of the beloved disciple to know You in the dark and say, "It is the Lord!" Give us the faith of Martha to confess, "You are the Christ, the Son of the living God." Give us the faith of Mary Magdalen to fall at Your feet crying, "Rabboni, Master."

Give us the faith of all Your saints, to whom the Blessed Sacrament has been Heaven begun on earth. In every Communion increase our faith; for with faith, the gifts of love, humility, reverence, and all good will come into our souls. Dearest Lord, please increase our faith. Amen.

EUCHARISTIC ASPIRATIONS

"Come to me, all you who labor and are burdened,
and I will give you rest."
— MATTHEW 11:28

"I am the living bread that came down from heaven;
whoever eats this bread will live forever; and the bread
that I will give is my flesh for the life of the world."
—JOHN 6:51

Jesus said to them, "Amen, amen, I say to you, unless you eat
the flesh of the Son of Man and drink his blood, you do not
have life within you. Whoever eats my flesh and drinks my
blood has eternal life, and I will raise him on the last day. For
my flesh is true food, and my blood is true drink. Whoever eats
my flesh and drinks my blood remains in me and I in him. Just
as the living Father sent me and I have life because of the
Father, so also the one who feeds on me will have life because
of me. This is the bread that came down from heaven.
Unlike your ancestors who ate and still died,
whoever eats this bread will live forever."
—JOHN 6:53-58

"Amen, amen, I say to you, whoever believes has eternal life."
—JOHN 6:47

Truly with you God is hidden,
the God of Israel, the savior!
—ISAIAH 45:15

LITANY OF THE SACRED HEART

Lord, have mercy. Lord, have mercy.

Christ, have mercy. Christ, have mercy.

Lord, have mercy. Lord, have mercy.

Christ hear us. Christ graciously hear us.

God the Father of heaven, R. Have mercy on us.

God the Son, Redeemer of the world,

God the Holy Spirit,

Holy Trinity, one God,

Heart of Jesus, Son of the Eternal Father,

Heart of Jesus, formed by the Holy Spirit in the womb of the Virgin Mother,

Heart of Jesus, substantially united to the Word of God,

Heart of Jesus, of infinite majesty,

Heart of Jesus, holy Temple of God,

Heart of Jesus, Tabernacle of the Most High,

Heart of Jesus, House of God and Gate of Heaven,

Heart of Jesus, glowing furnace of charity,

Heart of Jesus, source of justice and love,

Heart of Jesus, full of goodness and love,

Heart of Jesus, well-spring of all virtues,

Heart of Jesus, most worthy of all praise,

Heart of Jesus, King and center of all hearts,

Heart of Jesus, in Whom are all the treasures of wisdom and knowledge,

Heart of Jesus, in Whom dwells all the fullness of the Divinity,

Heart of Jesus, in Whom the Father is well pleased,

Heart of Jesus, of Whose fullness we have all received,

Heart of Jesus, desire of the everlasting hills, R. Have mercy on us.

Heart of Jesus, patient and rich in mercy,

Heart of Jesus, rich to all who invoke Thee,

Heart of Jesus, fount of life and holiness,

Heart of Jesus, atonement for our sins,

Heart of Jesus, overwhelmed with insults,

Heart of Jesus, bruised for our offenses,

Heart of Jesus, made obedient unto death,

Heart of Jesus, pierced with a lance,

Heart of Jesus, source of all consolation,

Heart of Jesus, our life and resurrection,

Heart of Jesus, our peace and reconciliation,

Heart of Jesus, victim for our sins,

Heart of Jesus, salvation of those who hope in Thee,

Heart of Jesus, hope of those who die in Thee,

Heart of Jesus, delight of all the saints,

Lamb of God, Who takes away the sins of the world,

Spare us, O Lord!

Lamb of God, Who takes away the sins of the world,

Graciously hear us, O Lord!

Lamb of God, Who takes away the sins of the world,

Have mercy on us!

V. Jesus, meek and humble of Heart.

R. Make our hearts like unto Thine.

Let us pray: Father, we rejoice in the gifts of love we have received from the heart of Jesus Your Son. Open our hearts to share His life and continue to bless us with His love. We ask this in the name of Jesus the Lord. Amen.

THE 12 PROMISES
OF THE SACRED HEART OF JESUS

Jesus revealed many promises to Saint Margaret Mary for those who would devote themselves to His Sacred Heart. Of these, the principal ones are as follows:

1. I will give them all the graces necessary for their state of life.
2. I will give peace in their families.
3. I will console them in all their troubles.
4. I will be their refuge in life and especially in death.
5. I will abundantly bless all their undertakings.
6. Sinners shall find in My Heart the source and infinite ocean of mercy.
7. Lukewarm souls shall become fervent.
8. Fervent souls shall rise speedily to great perfection.
9. I will bless those places wherein the image of My Sacred Heart shall be exposed and venerated.
10. I will give to priests the power to touch the most hardened hearts.
11. Persons who propagate this devotion shall have their names eternally written in My Heart.
12. In the excess of the mercy of My Heart, I promise you that My all powerful love will grant to all those who will receive Communion on the First Fridays, for nine consecutive months, the grace of final repentance: they will not die in My displeasure, nor without receiving the sacraments; and My Heart will be their secure refuge in that last hour.

THE FIRST FRIDAY DEVOTION

When Jesus appeared to Saint Margaret Mary, He asked her to receive Holy Communion on the first Friday of every month in order to make reparation, as much as she could, for the disrespect shown to the Blessed Sacrament during the previous month. One Friday, after she had received Holy Communion, He also gave her what is often called His greatest promise: "In the excess of the mercy of My Heart, I promise you that My all powerful love will grant to all those who will receive Communion on the First Fridays, for nine consecutive months, the grace of final repentance: they will not die in My displeasure, nor without receiving the sacraments; and My Heart will be their secure refuge in that last hour."

Saint Margaret Mary then made every effort to share this First Friday devotion with others, recommending especially that people would attend Mass and Communion and consecrate themselves to Jesus in His Most Sacred Heart on the first Friday of each month. Pope Leo XIII upheld this devotion and encouraged the faithful to practice it, granting special indulgences and privileges to those who would make the nine First Fridays.

REPARATION TO THE SACRED HEART

Now I rejoice in my sufferings for your sake,
and in my flesh I am filling up what is lacking in the afflictions
of Christ on behalf of his body, which is the church.
—COLOSSIANS 1:24

In His great love and mercy for us, God completely redeemed us from sin and its penalty of eternal death through the Passion, Death, and Resurrection of His Son, Jesus Christ.

Even so, He invites us to partake in His suffering for the sake of the others — His Body, the Church. We honor God with our worship and praise, but also by giving Him satisfaction for our many sins of commission and omission. Saint Paul urges us "to offer your bodies as a living sacrifice, holy and pleasing to God, your spiritual worship" (ROMANS 12:1).

When Jesus showed Saint Margaret Mary His Heart on fire with love and bearing the symbols of His Passion, He wanted us to know both the infinite malice of sin and the infinite love He has for us, so we could make an ardent return of love to Him, through a Communion of Reparation regularly, through a Holy Hour when possible, and through the offering of our daily life and prayers. These can console Christ since they are acts of love offered by His beloved to Him.

We are the Body of Christ, and members of one another. If one part of us suffers, we all suffer, and if one part is honored, we all share its joy. Therefore Jesus calls us to make reparation to His Sacred Heart, and to console Him for all He suffered to save us, to justify us, to sanctify us, and to glorify us. In a word, reparation is another way to say, "Thank You!"

LITANY OF THE BLESSED VIRGIN MARY

Litany of Loreto

Lord, have mercy on us. Christ, have mercy on us.
Lord, have mercy on us.
Christ, hear us. Christ graciously hear us.
God the Father of Heaven, R. Have mercy on us.
God the Son, Redeemer of the world,
God the Holy Spirit,
Holy Trinity, One God,

Holy Mary, R. Pray for us.
Holy Mother of God,
Holy Virgin of virgins,
Mother of Christ,
Mother of divine grace,
Mother most pure,
Mother most chaste,
Mother inviolate,
Mother undefiled,
Mother most amiable,
Mother most admirable,
Mother of good counsel,
Mother of our Creator,
Mother of our Redeemer,
Mother of the Church,
Virgin most prudent,
Virgin most venerable,

Virgin most renowned, R. Pray for us.
Virgin most powerful,
Virgin most merciful,
Virgin most faithful,
Mirror of justice,
Seat of wisdom,
Cause of our joy,
Spiritual vessel,
Vessel of honor,
Singular vessel of devotion,
Mystical rose,
Tower of David,
Tower of ivory,
House of gold,
Ark of the Covenant,
Gate of Heaven,
Morning star,
Health of the sick,
Refuge of sinners,
Comforter of the afflicted,
Help of Christians,
Queen of angels,
Queen of patriarchs,
Queen of prophets,
Queen of apostles,
Queen of martyrs,
Queen of confessors,
Queen of virgins,

Queen of all saints, R. Pray for us.
Queen conceived without original sin,
Queen assumed into heaven,
Queen of the most holy rosary,
Queen of families,
Queen of peace,

Lamb of God, Who takes away the sins of the world,
Spare us, O Lord!
Lamb of God, Who takes away the sins of the world,
Graciously hear us, O Lord!
Lamb of God, Who takes away the sins of the world,
Have mercy on us!

V. Pray for us, O Holy Mother of God.
R. That we may be made worthy of the promises of Christ.

Let us pray: Grant, we beseech You, O Lord God, that we Your servants may enjoy perpetual health of mind and body, and, by the glorious intercession of the Blessed Mary, ever Virgin, be delivered from present sorrow and enjoy eternal happiness. Through Christ, Our Lord. Amen.

THE SAINTS AND THE BLESSED SACRAMENT

"Christ held Himself in His hands when He gave His Body to His disciples saying: 'This is My Body.' No one partakes of this Flesh before he has adored it."

—Saint Augustine

"What wonderful majesty! What stupendous condescension! O sublime humility! That the Lord of the whole universe, God and the Son of God, should humble Himself like this under the form of a little bread, for our salvation. ... In this world I cannot see the Most High Son of God with my own eyes, except for His Most Holy Body and Blood."

—Saint Francis of Assisi

I hunger for the bread of God, the flesh of Jesus Christ ... I long to drink of his blood, the gift of unending love.

—Saint Ignatius of Antioch

"If Christ did not want to dismiss the Jews without food in the desert for fear that they would collapse on the way, it was to teach us that it is dangerous to try to get to heaven without the Bread of Heaven."

—Saint Jerome

"I throw myself at the foot of the Tabernacle like a dog at the foot of his Master."

—Saint John Vianney

"Aside from the Blessed Virgin, Saint Joseph was the first and most perfect adorer of Our Lord."

—Saint Peter Julian Eymard

"To the Father Christ entrusts His supreme desire: that all those whom He loves may be one in the same communion."

—Pope John Saint Paul II at Paris World Youth Day, 1997

"You come to me and unite Yourself intimately to me under the form of nourishment. Your Blood now runs in mine; Your Soul, Incarnate God, compenetrates mine, giving courage and support. What miracles! Who would have ever imagined such!"

—Saint Maximilian Kolbe

"The guest of our soul knows our misery; He comes to find an empty tent within us—that is all He asks. ... It is not to remain in a golden ciborium that He comes down each day from Heaven, but to find another Heaven, the Heaven of our soul in which He takes delight."

—Saint Therese of Lisieux

"Without the constant presence of our Divine Master upon the altar in my poor chapels, I never could have persevered casting my lot with the lepers of Molokai, the foreseen consequence of which begins now to appear on my skin, and is felt throughout the body. Holy Communion being the daily bread of a priest, I feel myself happy, well pleased, and resigned in the rather exceptional circumstances in which it has pleased Divine Providence to put me."

—Blessed Damien of Molokai, Apostle of the Lepers

"The time you spend with Jesus in the Blessed Sacrament is the best time you will spend on earth. Each moment that you spend with Jesus will deepen your union with Him and make your soul everlastingly more glorious and beautiful in Heaven, and will help bring about everlasting peace on earth."

—Blessed Teresa of Calcutta

SAINT JOSEPH AND THE BLESSED SACRAMENT

By Saint Peter Julian Eymard

Words cannot express the perfection of his adoration. If Saint John leaped in the womb at the approach of Mary, what feelings must have coursed through Joseph during those six months when he had at his side and under his very eyes the hidden God! ... How fervent that adoration must have been: My Lord and my God, behold your servant! No one can describe the adoration of this noble soul. He saw nothing, yet he believed; his faith had to pierce the virginal veil of Mary. So likewise with you! Under the veil of the Sacred Species your faith must see our Lord. Ask Saint Joseph for his lively, constant faith.

At Nazareth, Joseph's days were filled with work which necessarily took him away at times from his Infant God. During these hours Mary replaced him, but when evening brought him home again, he would pass the entire night in adoration, never tiring, only too happy for the chance to contemplate the hidden riches of Jesus' divinity. For he pierced the rough garments the Child wore, until his faith touched the Sacred Heart. In profound adoration he united himself to the special grace of each event in the life of Jesus. He adored our Lord in His hidden life and in His Passion and Death; he adored in advance the Eucharistic Christ in His tabernacles: there was nothing that our Lord could hide from Saint Joseph.

Among the graces which Jesus gave to His foster-father—and He flooded him with the graces attached to every one of His mysteries—is that grace which is special to an adorer of the Blessed Sacrament. That is the one we must ask of Saint Joseph. Have confidence, strong confidence in him. Take him as the patron and the model of your life of adoration.

Prayer for Priests

O Illustrious Patriarch Saint Joseph, who carried the Infant Jesus in your blessed arms and who, during the space of thirty years, lived in the most intimate familiarity with Him, take under your powerful protection those whom He has clothed with His authority and honored with the dignity of His priesthood, whom He has charged to continue His mission, to preach His Gospel, and to dispense everywhere His graces and blessings. Sustain them in their fatigues and labors; console them in their pains; fortify them in their combats; but above all, keep far from them all the evils of sin.

Obtain for them the humility of Saint John the Baptist, the faith of Saint Peter, the zeal and charity of Saint Paul, the purity of Saint John, and the spirit of prayer and recollection of which you, my dear Saint, are the model. After having been on earth, may they, the faithful dispensers of the Mysteries of your foster Son, Our Lord Jesus Christ, receive in Heaven the rewards promised to pastors according to the Heart of God. Amen.

THE SOULS IN PURGATORY AND THE BLESSED SACRAMENT

"O Holy Host, You who break down the gates of Purgatory and open the door of the Kingdom of Heaven to the Faithful!"
—SAINT PETER DAMIEN

Purgatory is the state of those who die as friends of God, assured of their eternal salvation, yet still needing purification to enter the bliss of heaven. Because we are one Body in Christ—the communion of saints— we who are on earth can help the souls in Purgatory through our prayers, most especially Holy Mass and Eucharistic Adoration. We can also help them through our almsgiving, indulgences, and works of penance. Saint Jerome asserted that every time we celebrate Mass devoutly, many souls are released from Purgatory, refreshed by the Body and Blood of the Lord offered for them. We can do everything for these souls and they can do everything for us.

Prayer for the Holy Souls of Purgatory

Our Lord dictated the following prayer to Saint Gertrude the Great to release 1,000 Souls from Purgatory each time it is prayed.

Eternal Father, I offer You the most precious Blood of Your Divine Son, Jesus, in union with the Masses said throughout the world today, for all the holy souls in Purgatory, for sinners everywhere, for sinners in the universal Church, those in my own home, and within my family. Amen.

Prayer for Deceased Parents

O God, Who has commanded us to honor our father and our mother, in Your mercy have pity on the souls of my father and mother, and forgive them their trespasses. Please help me to see them again in the joy of everlasting brightness. Through Christ our Lord. Amen.

Efficacious Prayer for the Faithful Departed

O Most compassionate Jesus, have mercy on the souls detained in Purgatory, for whose redemption You took upon Yourself our nature and endured a bitter death. Mercifully hear their sighs, look with pity upon the tears which they now shed before You, and by virtue of Your Passion, release them from the pains due to their sins. O most merciful Jesus, let Your Precious Blood reach down into Purgatory and refresh and revive the captive souls who suffer there. Stretch out to them Your strong right hand, and bring them forth into the place of refreshment, light, and peace. Amen.

Prayer for the Souls in Purgatory

O God, thank You so much for the gift of my life, my faith, my vocation, and for all the gifts You have so generously given me, from the least to the greatest. Please accept these prayers which I offer for all the holy souls in Purgatory: *Pray 7 times each: The Our Father, Hail Mary, Glory Be, and the Apostles' Creed.*

"We have to do the works of the one who sent me while it is day. Night is coming when no one can work." –JOHN 9:4

PRAYER FOR THE INDWELLING
OF THE SPIRIT
By Saint Augustine

Holy Spirit, powerful Consoler, sacred Bond of the Father and the Son, Hope of the afflicted, descend into my heart and establish in it Your loving dominion. Enkindle in my tepid soul the fire of Your love so that I may be wholly subject to You. We believe that when You dwell in us, you also prepare a dwelling for the Father and the Son. Please, therefore, come to me, Consoler of abandoned souls, and Protector of the needy. Help the afflicted, strengthen the weak, and support the wavering. Come and purify me. Let no evil desire take possession of me. You love the humble and resist the proud. Come to me, glory of the living, and hope of the dying. Lead me by Your grace that I may always be pleasing to You. Amen.

PRAYER ENTRUSTING THE CHURCH
TO MARY
By Pope Benedict XVI

Holy Mary, Mother of God,
you have given the world its true light,
Jesus, your Son—the Son of God.
You abandoned yourself completely
to God's call, and thus became a wellspring
of the goodness which flows forth from him.
Show us Jesus. Lead us to him.
Teach us to know and love him,
so that we too can become
capable of true love
and be fountains of living water
in the midst of a thirsting world. Amen.

PSALM 130-DE PROFUNDIS

Out of the depths I call to you, LORD;
Lord, hear my cry!
May your ears be attentive
to my cry for mercy.
If you, LORD, mark our sins,
Lord, who can stand?
But with you is forgiveness
and so you are revered.
I wait with longing for the LORD,
my soul waits for his word.
My soul looks for the Lord
more than sentinels for daybreak.
More than sentinels for daybreak,
let Israel look for the LORD,
For with the LORD is kindness,
with him is full redemption,
And God will redeem Israel
from all their sins.